FIRST 50
CAMPFIRE SO

YOU SHOULD STRUM ON GUITAR

ISBN 978-1-70514-683-5

Visit Hal Leonard Online at
www.halleonard.com

World headquarters, contact:
Hal Leonard
7777 West Bluemound Road
Milwaukee, WI 53213
Email: info@halleonard.com

In Europe, contact:
Hal Leonard Europe Limited
1 Red Place
London, W1K 6PL
Email: info@halleonardeurope.com

In Australia, contact:
Hal Leonard Australia Pty. Ltd.
4 Lentara Court
Cheltenham, Victoria, 3192 Australia
Email: info@halleonard.com.au

CONTENTS

Amie

Words and Music by Craig Fuller

Melody:

I can see why you think you be - long_ to me. _

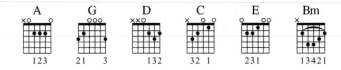

A   G   D   C   E   Bm

123   21 3   132   32 1   231   13421

Key of A

Intro
Moderately, in 2

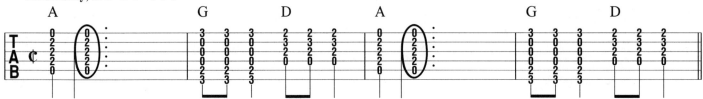

Verse 1

  A   **G**   **D**   **A**   **G**   **D**
I can see why you think you be-long to me.
  A   **G**   **D**
I never tried to make you think
    A   **D**
Or let you see one thing for your-self.
             C   **D**
But now you're off with someone else, and I'm a-lone.
        C   **E**
You see, I thought that I might keep you for my own.

Chorus

  A **G**   **D**
    Amie, what you wanna do?
  A   **G**   **D**
    I think I could stay with you
    Bm   **E**
For a while, maybe longer if I do. ***(Repeat Intro)***

Verse 2

Don't you think the time is right for us to find,
All the things we thought weren't proper
Could be right in time and can you see
Which way we should turn together or alone?
I can never see what's right or what is wrong
Until you take too long to see. ***(Repeat Chorus/Intro)***

Verse 3

Now it's come to what you want, you've had your way.
And all the things you thought before
Just faded into gray and can you see
That I don't know if it's you or if it's me?
If it's one of us I'm sure we both will see.
Won't ya look at me and tell me... ***(Repeat Chorus)***

Bad Moon Rising

Words and Music by John Fogerty

Melody:

I see a bad___ moon _ ris - in'.

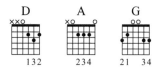

D   A   G

Key of D

Intro
Moderately fast

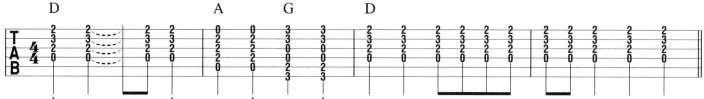

Verse 1

D   A   G   D
I see a bad moon risin'.
    A   G   D
I see trouble on the way.
    A   G   D
I see earth-quakes and lightnin'.
    A   G   D
I see bad times to-day.

Chorus

G
Don't go around tonight;
         D
Well, it's bound to take your life.
A   G   D
There's a bad moon on the rise.

Verse 2

I hear hurricanes a blowin'.
I know the end is comin' soon.
I fear rivers overflowin'.
I hear the voice of rage and ruin.   *(Repeat Chorus)*

Verse 3

Hope you got your things together.
Hope you are quite prepared to die.
Looks like we're in for nasty weather.
One eye is taken for an eye.   *(Repeat Chorus)*

Best of My Love

Words and Music by Don Henley,
Glenn Frey and John David Souther

Melody:

Ev - er - y night__   I'm ly - in' in bed____

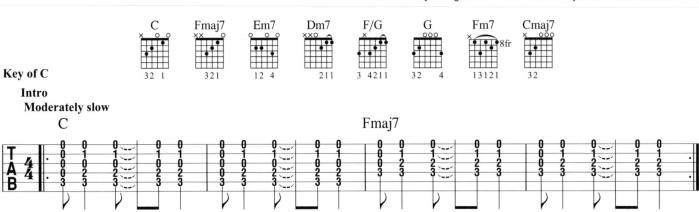

C   Fmaj7   Em7   Dm7   F/G   G   Fm7   Cmaj7

Key of C

Intro
Moderately slow

Verse 1

C   Fmaj7
Every night I'm lyin' in bed, holdin' you close in my dreams.
C   Fmaj7
Thinkin' about all the things that we said and comin' apart at the seams.
Em7   Dm7   Em7   F/G
  We tried to talk it over but the words come out too rough.
  C   Fmaj7   C   G
I know you were tryin' to give me the best of your love.

Verse 2

Beautiful faces, and loud empty places; look at the way that we live.
Wastin' our time on cheap talk and wine left us so little to give.
The same old crowd was like a cold, dark cloud that we could never rise above.
But here in my heart, I give you the best of my love.

Chorus

              C
‖: Whoa, ho, ho, ho, sweet darlin',
   Fmaj7
     You get the best of my love.   :‖

Bridge

Fm7   Cmaj7
Oo, I'm goin' back in time and it's a sweet dream.
        Fm7
It was a quiet night, and I would be alright,
        Dm7 G
If I could go on sleeping.

Verse 3

But every morning, I wake up and worry; what's gonna happen today.
You see it your way, and I see it mine. But we both see it slippin' away.
You know, we always had each other, baby. I guess that wasn't enough.
Oh, but here in my heart I give you the best of my love.   *(Repeat Chorus)*

Blowin' in the Wind

Words and Music by Bob Dylan

Melody:

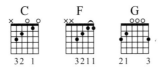

How man-y roads must a man_

Key of C

Moderately fast, in 2

Verse 1

    C   F   C
How many roads must a man walk down
             F   G
Before you call him a man?
C   F   C
How many seas must a white dove sail
             F   G
Before she sleeps in the sand?
           C   F   C
Yes, and how many times must the cannonballs fly
             F   G
Before they are forever banned?

Chorus

     F   G   C   F
The answer, my friend, is blowin' in the wind.
            G   C
The answer is blowin' in the wind.

Verse 2

How many years can a mountain exist
Before it is washed to the sea?
How many years can some people exist
Before they're allowed to be free?
Yes, and how many times can a man turn his head
And pretend that he just doesn't see?   ***(Repeat Chorus)***

Verse 3

How many times must a man look up
Before he can see the sky?
How many ears must one man have
Before he can hear people cry?
Yes, and how many deaths will it take till he knows
That too many people have died? ***(Repeat Chorus)***

Brown Eyed Girl

Words and Music by Van Morrison

Hey, where did we go

Key of G

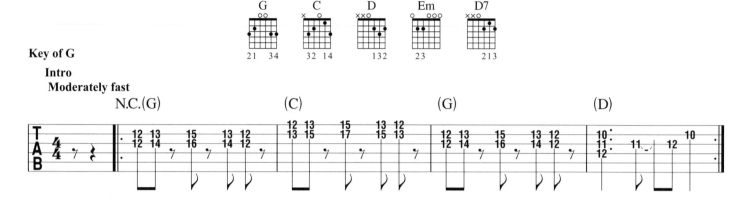

Intro
Moderately fast

Verse 1

```
G              C     G         D
  Hey, where did we go   days when the rain came?
G          C       G        D
  Down in the hollow,   playin' a new game.
G              C          G           D
  Laughing and a running, hey, hey,   skipping and a jumping.
G               C           G         D
  In the misty morning fog with   our, our hearts a thumpin'
   C        D          G      D
And you,    my brown-eyed girl.
```

Verse 2

```
  Now, whatever happened to Tuesday and so slow?
  Going down the old mine with a transistor radio.
  Standing in the sunlight laughing, hiding behind a rainbow's wall.
  Slipping and a sliding all along the waterfall
      C     D          G     Em
With you     my brown-eyed girl.
C          D        G
  You, my     brown-eyed girl.
D7
  Do you remember when we used to sing?
```

Chorus

```
G            C       G         D7
  Sha, la, la, la, la, la, la, la, la, la, la, tee, da. Just like that.
G            C       G         D7      G
  Sha, la, la, la, la, la, la, la, la, la, la, tee, da. La, tee, da.
```

Verse 3

```
So hard to find my way, now that I'm all on my own.
I saw you just the other day; my, how you have grown.
Cast my mem'ry back there, Lord.
Sometimes, I'm overcome thinkin' 'bout it.
Makin' love in the green grass behind the stadium with you,
My brown-eyed girl.
Do you remember when we used to sing?   (Repeat Chorus)
```

California Dreamin'

Words and Music by John Phillips
and Michelle Phillips

Melody:

All the leaves are brown

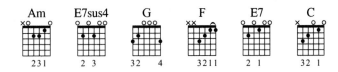

Am   E7sus4   G   F   E7   C

231   2 3   32 4   3211   2 1   32 1

Key of Am

Intro
Moderately slow

Am   E7sus4

(guitar tab)

Verse 1

      Am   **G**   **F**
All the leaves are brown,
    G   **E7sus4**   **E7**
And the sky is grey.
F   **C**   **E7**   **Am**
I've been for a walk
     F   **E7sus4**   **E7**
On a winter's day.
      Am   **G**   **F**
I'd be safe and warm
    G   **E7sus4**   **E7**
If I was in L.-A.
      Am   **G**   **F**
California dreamin'
  G   **E7sus4**
On such a winter's day.

Verse 2

Stopped in to a church I passed along the way.
Well, I got down on my knees and I pretend to pray.
You know the preacher liked the cold; he knows I'm gonna stay.
California dreamin' on such a winter's day.

Verse 3

All the leaves are brown, and the sky is grey.
I've been for a walk on a winter's day.
If I didn't tell her, I could leave today.
      Am   **G**   **F**   **G**
California dreamin'   on such a winter's...
Am **G**   **F**   **G**
Cali - fornia dream - in' on such a winter's...
Am **G**   **F**   **G**   **F**   **Am**
Cali - fornia dream - in' on such a winter's day.

Danny's Song

Words and Music by Kenny Loggins

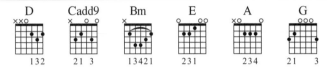

Key of D

Moderately slow, in 2

Verse 1

```
D              Cadd9      Bm
   People smile and tell me I'm the lucky one,
              E                    A
And we've just begun; think I'm gonna have a son.
D              Cadd9      Bm
   He will be like she and me, as free as a dove.
        E                    A
Con-ceived in love; sun is gonna shine above.
```

Chorus

```
G                    A
   And even though we ain't got money,
D       Bm
   I'm so in love with ya, honey,
   G         A         D      Bm
And ev'rything will bring a chain of love.
G                    A
   And in the morning when I rise,
D              Cadd9
   You bring a tear of joy to my eyes,
   Bm   E    A
And tell me ev'ry - thing is gonna be alright.
```

Verse 2

```
Seems as though a month ago I was Beta Chi.
Never got high; oh, was a sorry guy.
And now a smile, a face, a girl that shares my name.
Now I'm through with the game; this boy will never be the same.    (Repeat Chorus)
```

Verse 3

```
Pisces, Virgo rising is a very good sign.
Strong and kind, and the little boy is mine.
Now I see a family where there once was none.
Now we've just begun. Yeah, we're going to fly to the sun.    (Repeat Chorus)
```

Verse 4

```
Love the girl who holds the world in a paper cup;
Drink it up. Love her and she'll bring you luck.
And if you find she helps your mind, buddy, take her home.
Don't you live alone; try to earn what lovers own.    (Repeat Chorus)
```

Don't Worry, Be Happy

Words and Music by Bobby McFerrin

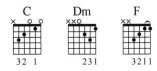

Key of C

Intro/Whistle Solo

Moderately

Verse 1

C
    Here's a little song I wrote.
    Dm
You might want to sing it note-for-note.
     F   **C**
Don't worry, be happy.

In ev'ry life we have some trouble,
Dm
    But when you worry, you make it double.
     F   **C**
Don't worry, be happy.   *(Repeat Intro)*

Verse 2

    Ain't got no place to lay your head.
    Somebody came and took your bed.
    Don't worry, be happy.
    The landlord say your rent is late.
    He may have to litigate.
    Don't worry, be happy.   *(Repeat Intro)*

Verse 3

    Ain't got no cash, ain't got no style.
    Ain't got no gal to make you smile.
    But don't worry, be happy.
    'Cause when you worry your face will frown,
    And that will bring ev'rybody down.
    So don't worry, be happy.
    Don't worry, be happy now.   *(Repeat Intro)*

Drift Away

Words and Music by Mentor Williams

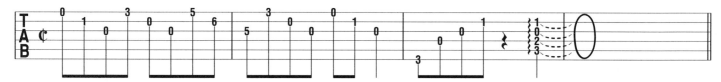

Key of C

Intro
Moderately, in 2

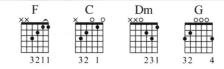

Verse 1

F   C
Day after day, I'm more con-fused,
F   C
Yet I look for the light through the pouring rain.
F   C
You know that's a game that I hate to lose.
Dm   F
And I'm feelin' the strain;   ain't it a shame?

Chorus

     C
‖: Oh, give me the beat, boys, and free my soul.
 G   F
I wanna get lost in your rock 'n roll and drift away.   :‖ *(Repeat Intro)*

Verse 2

Beginning to think that I'm wastin' time.
I don't understand the things I do.
The world outside looks so unkind.
Now, I'm countin' on you to carry me through. *(Repeat Chorus/Intro)*

Bridge

Dm
And when my mind is free,
F   C
You know a melody can move me.
Dm
And when I'm feelin' blue,
F   G
A guitar's comin' through to soothe me.

Verse 3

Thanks for the joy that you've given me.
I want you to know I believe in your song.
Rhythm and rhyme and harmony.
You help me along, makin' me strong. *(Repeat Chorus)*

Father and Son

Words and Music by Cat Stevens

Melody:

It's   not   time   to   make   a   change.

Key of G

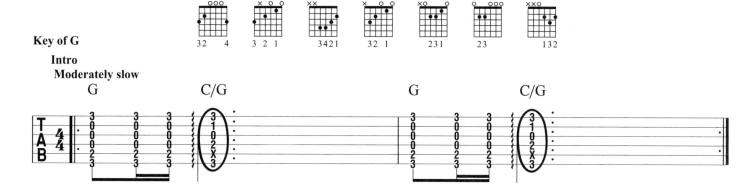

G   C/G   Bm   C   Am   Em   D

Intro
Moderately slow

G   C/G   G   C/G

Verse 1

     G   Bm   C   Am
It's not time to make a change. Just re-lax, take it easy.
     G   Em   Am   D
You're still young; that's your fault. There's so much you have to know.
     G   Bm   C   Am
Find a girl, settle down. If you want you can marry.
     G   Em   Am   D
Look at me. I am old but I'm happy.

Verse 2

I was once like you are now, and I know that it's not easy
To be calm when you found something going on.
But take your time. Think a lot. Think of everything you've got.
          G   Em   D   G C/G   G C/G
For you will still be here to-morrow but your dreams may not.

Verse 3

How can I try to explain? When I do he turns away again.
Well, it's always been the same, same old story.
From the moment I could talk I was ordered to listen.
Now there's a way and I know that I have to go away.

Verse 4

It's not time to make a change. Just sit down and take it slowly.
You're still young; that's your fault. There's so much you have to go through.
Find a girl, settle down. If you want you can marry.
Look at me. I am old but I'm happy.

Verse 5

All the times that I've cried, keeping all the things I knew inside.
And it's hard, but it's harder to ignore it.
If they were right, I'd agree. But it's them they know not me.
          G   Em   D   G   D   C   G
Now there's a way and I know that I have to go away. I know I have to go.

Five Hundred Miles

Words and Music by Hedy West

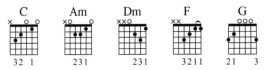

32 1   231   231   3211   21 3

Key of C

Moderately

Verse 1

          C   Am   Dm   F
If you miss the train I'm on, you will know that I am gone.
        Dm   G
You can hear the whistle blow a hundred miles.
            C   Am   Dm   F
A hundred miles, a hundred miles, a hundred miles, a hundred miles.
        Dm   G   C
You can hear the whistle blow a hundred miles.

Verse 2

Lord, I'm one, Lord, I'm two, Lord, I'm three, Lord, I'm four,
Lord, I'm five hundred miles from my home.
Five hundred miles, five hundred miles,
Five hundred miles, five hundred miles,
Lord, I'm five hundred miles from my home.

Verse 3

Not a shirt on my back, not a penny to my name,
Lord, I can't go a home this a way.
This a way, this a way, this a way, this a way,
Lord, I can't go a home this a way.

Outro-Verse

If you miss the train I'm on, you will know that I am gone;
You can hear the whistle blow a hundred miles.

Folsom Prison Blues

Words and Music by John R. Cash

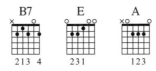

Key of E

Intro
Moderately, in 2

Verse 1

   E
I hear the train a comin'. It's rollin' 'round the bend.

And I ain't seen the sunshine since I don't know when.
   A   **E**
I'm stuck at Folsom Prison, and time keeps draggin' on.
   B7   **E**
But that train keeps a rollin' on down to San An-tone.

Verse 2

When I was just a baby, my mama told me, "Son,
Always be a good boy; don't ever play with guns."
But I shot a man in Reno just to watch him die.
When I hear that whistle blowin', I hang my head and cry.

Verse 3

I bet there's rich folks eatin' from a fancy dining car.
They're prob'ly drinkin' coffee and smokin' big cigars.
Well, I know I had it comin', I know I can't be free.
But those people keep a movin' and that's what tortures me.

Verse 4

Well, if they freed me from this prison, if that railroad train was mine,
I bet I'd move it on a little farther down the line.
Far from Folsom Prison, that's where I want to stay.
And I'd let that lonesome whistle blow my blues away.

Free Fallin'

**Words and Music by Tom Petty
and Jeff Lynne**

Melody:

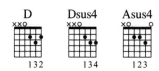

Key of D

Intro
Moderately slow

Verse 1

        D   Dsus4   D   Asus4
She's a good girl,   loves her mama.
        D   Dsus4   D   Asus4
Loves Je - sus, and Ameri-ca, too.
        D   Dsus4   D   Asus4
She's a good girl, crazy 'bout Elvis.
        D   Dsus4   D   Asus4
Loves hors-es and her boy-friend, too.   *(Repeat Intro)*

Verse 2

And it's a long day livin' in Reseda.
There's a freeway runnin' through the yard.
And I'm a bad boy 'cause I don't even miss her.
I'm a bad boy for breakin' her heart.

Chorus

        D   Dsus4   D   Asus4
‖: Now I'm free,
        D   Dsus4   D   Asus4
Free fallin'.   :‖

Verse 3

Now all the vampires walkin' through the valley
Move west down Ventura Boulevard.
And all the bad boys are standin' in the shadows.
And the good girls are home with broken hearts.   *(Repeat Chorus)*

Verse 4

I wanna glide down over Mulholland,
I wanna write her name in the sky.
I'm gonna free fall out into nothin',
Gonna leave this world for a while.   *(Repeat Chorus)*

The Gambler

Words and Music by Don Schlitz

Melody:

On a warm sum-mer's eve-nin'

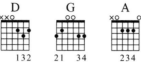

Key of D

Moderately

Verse 1

D   G   D
On a warm summer's evenin', on a train bound for nowhere,
               A
I met up with a gambler; we were both too tired to sleep.
D   G   D
So we took turns a starin' out the window at the darkness,
G   D A   D
Till boredom over-took us and he began to speak.

Verse 2

He said, "Son, I've made my life out of readin' people's faces
And knowin' what the cards were by the way they held their eyes.
So if you don't mind me sayin', I can see you're out of aces.
For a taste of your whiskey, I'll give you some advice."

Verse 3

So I handed him my bottle and he drank down my last swallow.
Then he bummed a cigarette and asked me for a light.
And the night got deathly quiet, and his face lost all expression.
Said, "If you're gonna play the game, boy, ya gotta learn to play it right."

Chorus

    D   G   D
"You got to know when to hold 'em, know when to fold 'em.
G   D   A
 Know when to walk away, know when to run.
    D G D   G   D
You never count your money when you're sittin' at the table.
       G   D A   D
There'll be time e-nough for countin' when the dealin's done.

Verse 4

"Now ev'ry gambler knows the secret to survivin'
Is knowin' what to throw away and knowin' what to keep.
'Cause ev'ry hand's a winner and ev'ry hand's a loser.
And the best you can hope for is to die in your sleep."

Verse 5

So when he finished speakin', he turned back toward the window,
Crushed out his cigarette and faded off to sleep.
Then somewhere in the darkness, the gambler, he broke even.
But in his final words I found an ace that I could keep. *(Repeat Chorus)*

Good Riddance
(Time of Your Life)

Words by Billie Joe
Music by Green Day

Melody:

An - oth - er turn - ing point, __

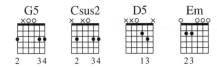

Key of G

Intro
Moderately slow

Verse 1

G5   Csus2   D5
Another turning point, a fork stuck in the road.
G5   Csus2   D5
Time grabs you by the wrist, di-rects you where to go.
Em   D5   Csus2   G5
So make the best of this test and don't ask why.
Em   D5   Csus2   G5
It's not a question, but a lesson learned in time.

Chorus

   Em   G
It's something unpre-dictable
   Em   G
But in the end is right.
   Em   D   G
I hope you had the time of your life.   *(Repeat Intro)*

Verse 2

So take the photographs and still frames in your mind.
Hang it on a shelf in good health and good time.
Tattoos of memories, and dead skin on trial.
For what it's worth, it was worth all the while.   *(Repeat Chorus)*

Hallelujah

Words and Music by Leonard Cohen

Now, I've heard there was a se - cret chord

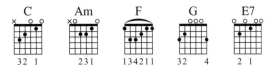

Key of C

Intro
Moderately slow

Verse 1

             C   Am
Now, I've heard there was a secret chord
      C   Am
That David played, and it pleased the Lord,
     F   G   C   G
But you don't really care for music, do ya?
     C   F   G
It goes like this, the fourth, the fifth,
        Am   F
The minor fall, the major lift.
      G   E7   Am
The baffled king com - posing "Halle - lujah."

Chorus

         F   Am
Halle - lujah! Halle - lujah!
         F   C G C   G
Halle - lujah! Halle - lu - jah!

Verse 2

Your faith was strong, but you needed proof.
You saw her bathing on the roof.
Her beauty and the moonlight overthrew ya.
She tied you to her kitchen chair,
She broke your throne and she cut your hair,
And from your lips she drew the hallelujah.   *(Repeat Chorus)*

Verse 3

You say I took the Name in vain,
I don't even know the Name,
But if I did, well, really, what's it to ya?
There's a blaze of light in ev'ry word,
It doesn't matter which you heard,
The holy or the broken hallelujah.   *(Repeat Chorus)*

Have You Ever Seen the Rain?

Words and Music by John Fogerty

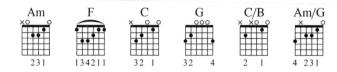

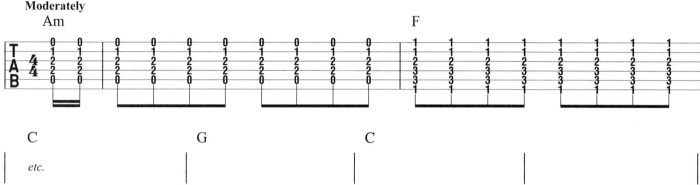

Key of C

Intro
Moderately

Verse 1

C
    Someone told me long ago, there's a calm before the storm.
G   **C**
I know, it's been coming for some time.

When it's over, so they say, it'll rain a sunny day.
G   **C**
I know, shining down like water.

Chorus

F   **G**   **C** **C/B**   **Am** **Am/G**
    I want to know, have you ever seen the rain?
F   **G**   **C** **C/B**   **Am** **Am/G**
    I want to know, have you ever seen the rain
F   **G**   **C**
    Coming down on a sunny day?

Verse 2

    Yesterday and days before, sun is cold and rain is hard.
    I know, been that way for all my time.
    Till forever on it goes, through the circle, fast and slow.
    I know, it can't stop, I wonder. *(Repeat Chorus)*

Hey Jude

Words and Music by John Lennon
and Paul McCartney

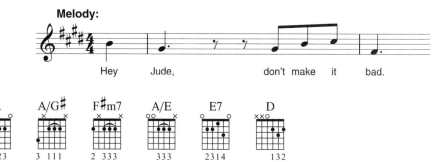

Key of E

Moderately

Verse 1

E   B7   E

Hey Jude, don't make it bad. Take a sad song and make it better.

A   E   B7   E

Re-member to let her into your heart, then you can start to make it bet-ter.

Verse 2

Hey Jude, don't make it bad. Take a sad song and make it better.
Remember to let her into your heart, then you can start to make it better.

Bridge

A   A/G♯   F♯m7   A/E   B7   E

And anytime you feel the pain, hey Jude, re-frain. Don't carry the world upon your shoul-ders.

A   A/G♯ F♯m7 A/E   B7   E

For well you know that it's a fool who plays it cool by making his world a little colder.

E7   B7

Na, na, na, na, na, na, na, na, na.

Verse 3

Hey Jude, don't let me down. You have found her, now go and get her.
Remember to let her into your heart, then you can start to make it better.

Bridge

So let it out and let it in. Hey Jude, begin. You're waiting for someone to perform with.
And don't you know that it's just you? Hey Jude, you'll do. The movement you need is on your shoulder.
Na, na, na, na, na, na, na, na, na.

Verse 4

Hey Jude, don't make it bad. Take a sad song and make it better.
Remember to let her under your skin, then you begin to make it better,
Better, better, better, better, better, oh.

Outro

E   D

‖: Na,   na, na, na, na, na, na,

A   E

Na, na, na, na. Hey Jude.   :‖

A Horse with No Name

Words and Music by Dewey Bunnell

Melody:

On the first part of the jour - ney,

Key of Em

Intro
Moderately

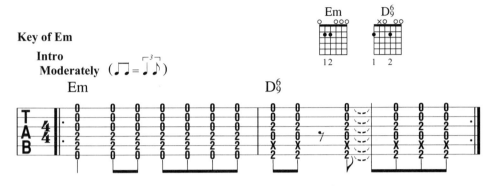

Verse 1

         Em   **D⁶₉**
On the first part of the journey,
         Em   **D⁶₉**
I was looking at all the life.
           Em   **D⁶₉**
There were plants and birds and rocks and things.
          Em   **D⁶₉**
There was sand and hills and rains.
       Em   **D⁶₉**
The first thing I met was a fly with a buzz
         Em   **D⁶₉**
And the sky with no clouds.
       Em   **D⁶₉**
The heat was hot and the ground was dry,
         Em   **D⁶₉**
But the air was full of sounds.

Chorus

       Em   **D⁶₉**
I've been through the desert on a horse with no name.
        Em   **D⁶₉**
It felt good to be out of the rain.
        Em   **D⁶₉**
In the desert you can re - member your name
          Em   **D⁶₉**
'Cause there ain't no one for to give you no pain.
Em **D⁶₉**   **Em** **D⁶₉**
‖: La, la, la, la, la, la. La, la, la. :‖

Verse 2

    After two days in the desert sun my skin began to turn red.
    After three days in the desert fun I was looking at a river bed.
    And the story it told of a river that flowed made me sad to think it was dead.   *(Repeat Chorus)*

Verse 3

    After nine days I let the horse run free 'cause the desert had turned to sea.
    There were plants and birds and rocks and things, there was sand and hills and rains.
    The ocean is a desert with its life underground and the perfect disguise above.
    Under the cities lies a heart made of ground but the humans will give no love.   *(Repeat Chorus)*

I Can See Clearly Now

Words and Music by Johnny Nash

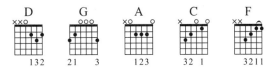

Key of D

Moderately

Verse 1

```
    D         G              D
    I can see clearly now, the rain is gone.
              G           A
    I can see all obstacles in my way.
    D         G              D
    Gone are the dark clouds that had me blind.
              C      G         D
‖: It's gonna be a bright, bright sunshiny day. :‖
```

Verse 2

I think I can make it now, the pain is gone.
All of the bad feelings have disappeared.
Here is that rainbow I've been praying for.
It's gonna be a bright, bright sunshiny day.

Bridge

```
    F                          C
    Look all around, there's nothing but blue skies.
    F                             A
    Look straight ahead, there's nothing but blue skies.
```

Verse 3

I can see clearly now, the rain is gone.
I can see all obstacles in my way.
Gone are the dark clouds that had me blind.

Outro

```
          C      G         D
‖: It's gonna be a bright, bright sunshiny day. :‖
```

I Walk the Line

Words and Music by John R. Cash

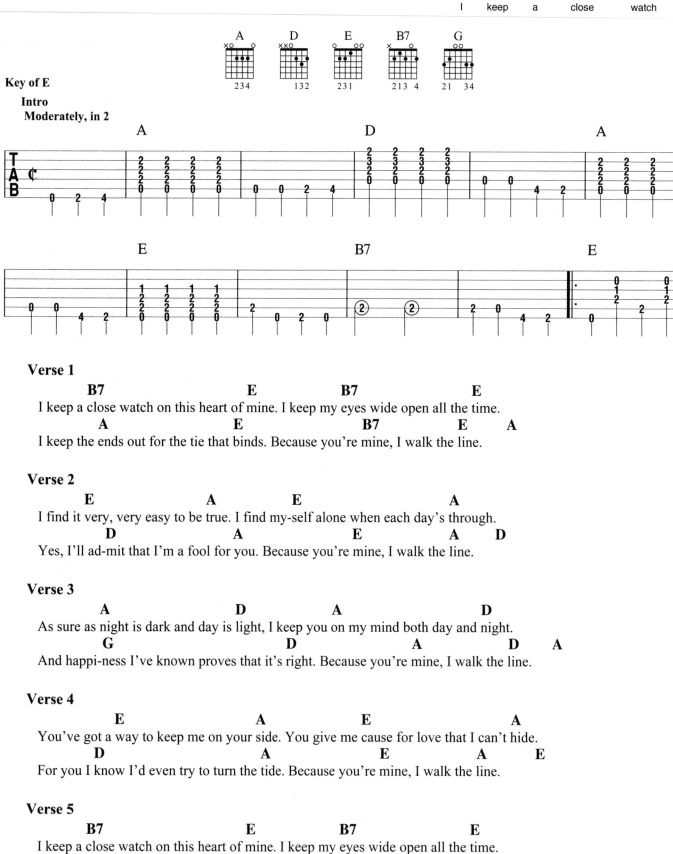

Key of E

Intro
Moderately, in 2

Verse 1

B7   E   B7   E

I keep a close watch on this heart of mine. I keep my eyes wide open all the time.

A   E   B7   E   A

I keep the ends out for the tie that binds. Because you're mine, I walk the line.

Verse 2

E   A   E   A

I find it very, very easy to be true. I find my-self alone when each day's through.

D   A   E   A   D

Yes, I'll ad-mit that I'm a fool for you. Because you're mine, I walk the line.

Verse 3

A   D   A   D

As sure as night is dark and day is light, I keep you on my mind both day and night.

G   D   A   D   A

And happi-ness I've known proves that it's right. Because you're mine, I walk the line.

Verse 4

E   A   E   A

You've got a way to keep me on your side. You give me cause for love that I can't hide.

D   A   E   A   E

For you I know I'd even try to turn the tide. Because you're mine, I walk the line.

Verse 5

B7   E   B7   E

I keep a close watch on this heart of mine. I keep my eyes wide open all the time.

A   E   B7   E

I keep the ends out for the tie that binds. Because you're mine, I walk the line.

I'd Like to Teach the World to Sing

Words and Music by Bill Backer, Roquel Davis,
Roger Cook and Roger Greenaway

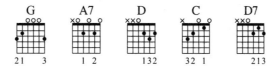

Key of G

Moderately slow

Verse 1

   G
I'd like to build the world a home,
    A7
And furnish it with love.
     D
Grow apple trees and honey bees
   C   **G**
And snow-white turtle doves.

Verse 2

I'd like to teach the world to sing in perfect harmony.
I'd like to hold it in my arms and keep it company.

Verse 3

I'd like to see the world, for once, all standing hand in hand,
And hear them echo through the hills for peace throughout the land.

Bridge

         G
That's the song I hear,
      A7   **D7**
Let the world sing to-day.

Outro

   G
I'd like to teach the world to sing
 A7   **D**   **D7** **G**
In perfect harmo-ny.

Island in the Sun

Words and Music by Rivers Cuomo

When you're on____ a hol - i - day,____

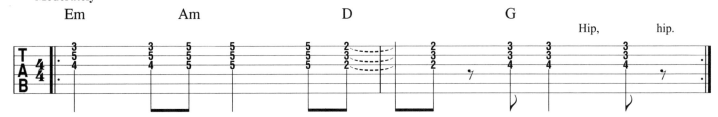

Key of G

Intro
Moderately

Hip,   hip.

Verse 1

  Em Am   D G Em
      When you're on a holi-day,
  Am   D   G   Em
     You can't find no words to say
  Am   D   G   Em
     All the things that come to you.
  Am   D   G
     And I want to feel it too.

Chorus

  Em Am   D   G   Em
      On an island in the sun,
  Am   D   G Em
     We'll be playing and having fun.
  Am   D   G Em
     And it makes me feel so fine,
  Am   D   G
  I can't con-trol my brain.   *(to Intro/Verse 2)*

Verse 2

  When you're on a golden sea,
  You don't need no memory.
  Just a place to call your own,
  As we drift into the zone.   *(Repeat Chorus)*

Bridge

  D   G
     We'll run a-way together.
  D   G
     We'll spend some time, forever.
  C   Am   D
     We'll never feel bad any-more. Hip, hip. *(Repeat Intro)*

Knockin' on Heaven's Door

Words and Music by Bob Dylan

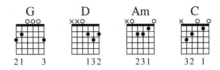

Ma - ma, take this badge off___ of me.

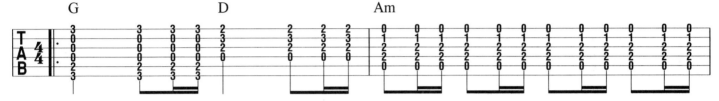

Key of G

Intro
Moderately slow

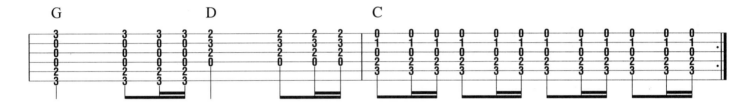

Verse 1

G   D   Am
   Mama, take this badge off of me.
G   D   C
   I can't use it any-more.
G   D   Am
   It's gettin' dark, too dark to see.
G   D   C
   I feel like I'm knockin' on heaven's door.

Chorus

G   D   Am
   Knock, knock, knockin' on heaven's door.
G   D   C
   Knock, knock, knockin' on heaven's door.
G   D   Am
   Knock, knock, knockin' on heaven's door.
G   D   C
   Knock, knock, knockin' on heaven's door.

Verse 2

   Mama, put my guns in the ground.
   I can't shoot them anymore.
   That long, black cloud is comin' down.
   I feel like I'm knockin' on heaven's door. *(Repeat Chorus)*

Leaving on a Jet Plane

Words and Music by John Denver

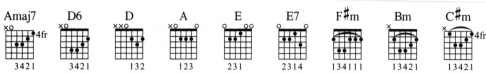

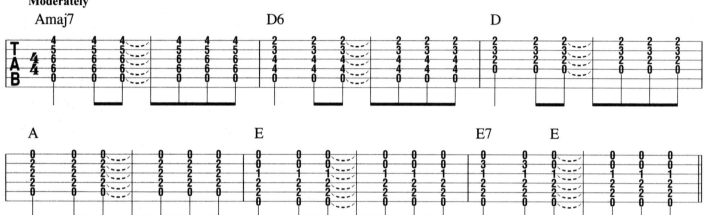

Key of A

Intro
Moderately

Amaj7   D6   D

A   E   E7   E

Verse 1

       Amaj7   **D6**   **Amaj7**   **D6**
All my bags are packed; I'm ready to go. I'm standing here out-side your door.

       Amaj7   **F#m**   **E**   **E7**
I hate to wake you up to say good-bye.

         Amaj7   **D6**   **Amaj7**   **D6**
But the dawn is breaking; it's early morn'. The taxi's waiting; he's blowing his horn.

       Amaj7   **F#m**   **E**
Al-ready I'm so lonesome I could cry.

Pre-Chorus

   A   **D**   **A**   **D**   **A**   **Bm**   **E**
So kiss me and smile for me. Tell me that you'll wait for me. Hold me like you'll never let me go.

Chorus

   A   **D**   **A**   **D**   **A**   **C#m**   **D6**   **E**
I'm leaving on a jet plane,   I don't know when I'll be back again.   Oh, babe, I hate to go.

Verse 2

There's so many times I've let you down, so many times I've played around.
I tell you now, they don't mean a thing.
Ev'ry place I go, I think of you. Ev'ry song I sing, I sing for you.
When I come back, I'll wear your wedding ring.   *(Repeat Chorus)*

Verse 3

Now the time has come to leave you. One more time, let me kiss you.
Then close your eyes; I'll be on my way.
Dream about the days to come, when I won't have to leave alone.
About the time I won't have to say... *(Repeat Chorus)*

Let It Be

Words and Music by John Lennon
and Paul McCartney

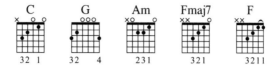

Key of C

Moderately

Verse 1

       C   G   Am   Fmaj7
When I find myself in times of trouble, Mother Mary comes to me,
C   G   F   C
Speaking words of wisdom. Let it be.
                  G   Am   Fmaj7
And in my hour of darkness, she is standing right in front of me,
C   G   F   C
Speaking words of wisdom. Let it be.

Chorus

       Am   G   Fmaj7 C
Let it be, let it be. Ah, let it be, let it be.
                  G   F   C
Whisper words of wisdom, let it be.

Verse 2

And when the broken-hearted people living in the world agree,
There will be an answer, let it be.
For though they may be parted, there is still a chance that they will see
There will be an answer, let it be.   ***(Repeat Chorus)***

Verse 3

And when the night is cloudy there is still a light that shines on me;
Shine until tomorrow, let it be.
I wake up to the sound of music. Mother Mary comes to me,
Speaking words of wisdom, let it be.   ***(Repeat Chorus)***

The Lion Sleeps Tonight

New Lyrics and Revised Music by
George David Weiss, Luigi Creatore
and Hugo Peretti

Wee, _____

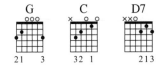

Key of G

Intro
Moderately slow

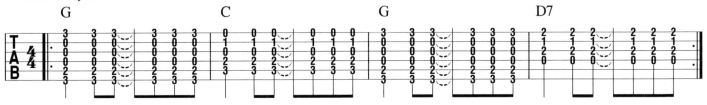

Verse 1

G   C
In the jungle, the mighty jungle,
    G   D7
The lion sleeps to-night.
G   C
In the jungle, the quiet jungle,
    G   D7
The lion sleeps to-night.

Chorus

G C G   D7
Wee,   ooh, wim-o-weh.
G C G   D7
Wee,   ooh, wim-o-weh.

Verse 2

Near the village, the peaceful village,
The lion sleeps tonight.
Near the village, the quiet village,
The lion sleeps tonight.   *(Repeat Chorus)*

Verse 3

Hush, my darling, don't fear, my darling,
The lion sleeps tonight.
Hush, my darling, don't fear, my darling,
The lion sleeps tonight.   *(Repeat Chorus)*

Mr. Tambourine Man

Words and Music by Bob Dylan

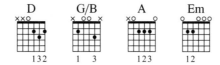

Hey,   Mis - ter Tam - bou - rine___ Man,

Key of D

Intro

Moderately fast

D

Chorus

G/B   A   D   G/B   D   G/B   A

Hey, Mr. Tambourine Man, play a song for me. I'm not sleepy and there is no place I'm going to.

G/B   A   D   G/B   D   G/B   A   D

Hey, Mr. Tambourine Man, play a song for me. In the jingle-jangle morning I'll come followin' you.

Verse 1

          G/B   A   D   G/B

Though I know that evenin's empire has returned into sand,

D   G/B   D   G/B Em   A

Vanished from my hand, left me blindly here to stand but still not sleeping.

    G/B   A   D   G/B D   G/B

My weariness a-mazes me, I'm branded on my feet. I have no one to meet,

        D   G/B   Em   A

And the ancient empty street's too dead for dreaming.   ***(Repeat Chorus)***

Verse 2

Take me on a trip upon your magic swirlin' ship. My senses have been stripped, my hands can't feel to grip.

My toes too numb to step, wait only for my boot heels to be wanderin'.

I'm ready to go anywhere, I'm ready for to fade into my own parade.

Cast your dancing spell my way; I promise to go under it.   ***(Repeat Chorus)***

Verse 3

Though you might hear laughin', spinnin', swingin' madly across the sun,

It's not aimed at anyone, it's just escapin' on the run. And but for the sky there are no fences facin'.

And if you hear vague traces of skippin' reels of rhyme to your tambourine in time, it's just a ragged clown behind.

I wouldn't pay it any mind. It's just a shadow you're seeing that he's chasing.   ***(Repeat Chorus)***

Verse 4

Then take me disappearin' through the smoke rings of my mind.

Down the foggy ruins of time, far past the frozen leaves,

The haunted, frightened trees, out to the windy beach, far from the twisted reach of crazy sorrow.

Yes, to dance beneath the diamond sky with one hand waving free.

Silhouetted by the sea, circled by the circus sands, with all the memory and fate driven deep beneath the waves.

Let me forget about today until tomorrow.   ***(Repeat Chorus)***

Mountain Dew

Words and Music by Scott Wiseman
and Bascom Lunsford

Melody:

Not___ ver - y far from me

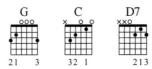

Key of G

Moderately

Verse 1

G
Not very far from me, there's an old hollow tree
      C   **G**
Where you lay down a dollar or two.

Then you go around the bend, then you come back again
                      D7   **G**
With a jug of that good old mountain dew.

Chorus

          G
Oh, they call it that old mountain dew,
 C   **G**
And them that refuse it are few.

Oh, I'll hush up my mug if you'll fill up my jug
           D7   **G**
With that good old mountain dew.

Verse 2

Now, the preacher came by, with his head h'isted high,
Said his wife had took down with the flu.
And he thought that we ought just to give her a snort
Of that good old mountain dew.   *(Repeat Chorus)*

Verse 3

Now, my Uncle Mort, he's sawed off and short,
And he measures 'bout four-foot-two.
But he thinks he's a giant when you give him a pint
Of that good old mountain dew.   *(Repeat Chorus)*

Ob-La-Di, Ob-La-Da

Words and Music by John Lennon
and Paul McCartney

Des-mond has a bar-row in the mar-ket - place, _

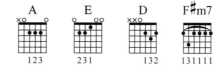

Key of A

Intro
Moderately

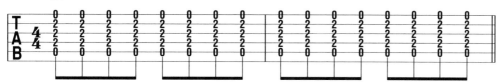

Verse 1

   A   E   A
Desmond has a barrow in the marketplace, Molly is the singer in a band.
                                   D   A   E   A
Desmond says to Molly, girl, I like your face, and Molly says this as she takes him by the hand.

Chorus

       A   E F#m7 A   E   A
‖: Ob-La-Di, Ob-La-Da, life goes on, bra,   la, la, how their life goes on.   :‖

Verse 2

Desmond takes a trolley to the jeweler's store, buys a twenty-carat golden ring.
Takes it back to Molly waiting at the door, and as he gives it to her, she begins to sing: *(Repeat Chorus)*

Bridge

D   A
In a couple of years, they have built a home sweet home.
D   A   E
With a couple of kids running in the yard of Desmond and Molly Jones.

Verse 3

Happy ever after in the marketplace, Desmond lets the children lend a hand.
Molly stays at home and does her pretty face, and in the evening she still sings it with the band.

Outro-Chorus

       A   E F#m7 A   E   A
‖: Ob-La-Di, Ob-La-Da, life goes on, bra,   la, la, how their life goes on.   :‖
                              E   A
And if you want some fun, take Ob-La-Di-Bla-Da.

Peaceful Easy Feeling

Words and Music by Jack Tempchin

Melody:

I like the way ___ your spark - ling ___

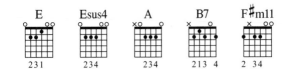

Key of E

Intro
Moderately

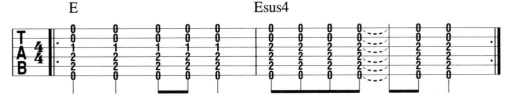

Verse 1

E   A   E   A
I like the way your sparkling earrings lay
E   A   B7
Against your skin so brown.
E   A   E   A
And I wanna sleep with you in the desert to-night,
E   A   B7
With a billion stars all a-round.

Chorus

           A   E
And I got a peaceful easy feeling,
A   F#m11   B7
And I know you won't let me down.
       E   F#m11 A   B7   E
'Cause I'm al - ready standing   on the ground.   *(Repeat Intro)*

Verse 2

And I found out a long time ago
What a woman can do for your soul.
Aw, but she can't take you any way
You don't already know how to go.   *(Repeat Chorus/Intro)*

Verse 3

I get this feeling I may know you
As a lover and a friend.
But this voice keeps whispering in my other ear,
Tells me, I may never see you again.   *(Repeat Chorus)*

Puff the Magic Dragon

Words and Music by Lenny Lipton and Peter Yarrow

Melody:

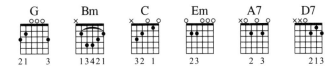

Puff the mag - ic drag - on...

G   Bm   C   Em   A7   D7

21 3   13421   32 1   23   2 3   213

Key of G

Moderately

Verse 1

G   Bm   C   G
Puff the magic dragon lived by the sea,
    C   G   Em   A7   D7
And frolicked in the autumn mist in a land called Hona-lee.
G   Bm   C   G
Little Jackie Paper loved that rascal Puff,
    C   G   Em   A7 D7 G   D7
And brought him strings and sealing wax and other fancy stuff. Oh,

Chorus

G   Bm   C   G
Puff the magic dragon lived by the sea
    C   G   Em   A7   D7
And frolicked in the autumn mist in a land called Hona-lee.
G   Bm   C   G
Puff the magic dragon lived by the sea
    C   G   Em   A7   D7   G   D7
And frolicked in the autumn mist in a land called Hona-lee.

Verse 2

Together they would travel on a boat with billowed sail.
Jackie kept a lookout perched on Puff's gigantic tail.
Noble kings and princes would bow whene'er they came.
Pirate ships would lower their flags when Puff roared out his name. Oh...　*(Repeat Chorus)*

Verse 3

A dragon lives forever, but not so little boys.
Painted wings and giant rings make way for other toys.
One gray night it happened; Jackie Paper came no more.
And Puff that mighty dragon, he ceased his fearless roar.

Verse 4

His head was bent in sorrow, green tears fell like rain.
Puff no longer went to play along the Cherry Lane.
Without his lifelong friend, Puff could not be brave.
So Puff that mighty dragon sadly slipped into his cave. Oh...　*(Repeat Chorus)*

Ring of Fire

Words and Music by Merle Kilgore
and June Carter

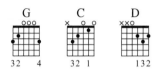

Melody:

Love   is a burn - ing   thing

G   C   D

Key of G

Intro
Moderately

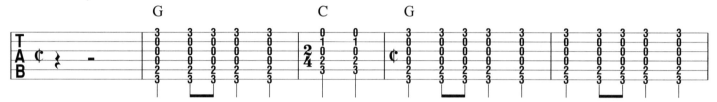

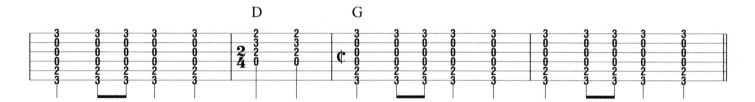

Verse 1

G   C   G   C G
Love is a burning thing
              D   G   D   G
And it makes a fiery ring.
           C   G   C G
Bound by wild de-sires,
        D   G
I fell into a ring of fire.

Chorus

D   C   G
I fell into a burning ring of fire.
     D
I went down, down, down
        C   G
And the flames went higher.

And it burns, burns, burns,
      C   G   D   G
The ring of fire, the ring of fire.   ***(Repeat Intro)***

Verse 2

The taste of love is sweet
When hearts like ours meet.
I fell for you like a child.
Oh, but the fire went wild.   ***(Repeat Chorus)***

Ripple

Words by Robert Hunter
Music by Jerry Garcia

Melody:

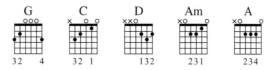

Key of G

Moderately

Verse 1

              G   C
If my words did glow with the gold of sunshine,
                                 G
And my tunes were played on the harp, un-strung,
                             C
Would you hear my voice come through the music?
G   D   C   G
Would you hold it near, as if it were your own?

Verse 2

It's a hand-me-down, the thoughts are broken.
Perhaps they're better left unsung.
I don't know. Don't really care.
Let there be songs to fill the air.

Chorus

Am   D
Ripple in still water,
                G   C
When there is no pebble tossed.
    A   D
No wind to blow.

Verse 3

Reach out your hand, if your cup be empty.
If your cup is full, may it be again.
Let it be known, there is a fountain
That was not made by the hands of man.

Verse 4

There is a road; no simple highway,
Between the dawn and the dark of night.
And if you go, no one may follow.
That path is for your steps alone.   *(Repeat Chorus)*

Verse 5

You who choose to lead must follow.
But if you fall, you fall alone.
If you stand, then who's to guide you?
If I knew the way, I would take you home.   *(Repeat Chorus)*

Rocky Mountain High

Words and Music by John Denver
and Mike Taylor

Melody:

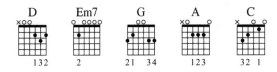

He was born ___ in the sum - mer

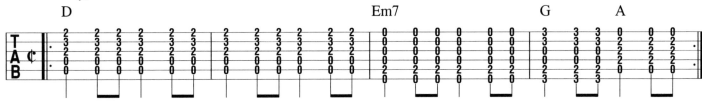

Key of D

Intro
Moderately, in 2

Verse 1

        D   **Em7**   **C** **A**
He was born in the summer of his twenty-seventh year,
        D   **Em7** **G** **A**
Comin' home to a place he'd never been before.
        D   **Em7**   **C** **A**
He left yesterday behind him; you might say he was born again.
        D   **Em7** **G** **A**
You might say he found a key for every door.

Verse 2

When he first came to the mountains, his life was far away.
On the road and hangin' by a song.
But the string's already broken and he doesn't really care.
It keeps changin' fast, and it don't last for long.

Chorus 1

        G   **A**   **D**
But the Colorado Rocky Mountain high,
        G   **A**   **D**
I've seen it rainin' fire in the sky.
        G   **A**   **D**   **G**
The shadow from the starlight is softer than a lulla-by.
                D   **Em7** **G**
Rocky Mountain high, Colo-rado.
        A   **D**   **Em7** **G** **A**
Rocky Mountain high, Colo-rado.

Verse 3

He climbed Cathedral Mountains, he saw silver clouds below.
He saw everything as far as you can see.
And they say that he got crazy once and he tried to touch the sun.
And he lost a friend but kept a memory.

Verse 4

Now he walks in quiet solitude, the forests and the streams.
Seeking grace in every step he takes.
His sight has turned inside himself to try and understand
The serenity of a clear blue mountain lake.

Chorus 2

And the Colorado Rocky Mountain high,
I've seen it rainin' fire in the sky.
Talk to God and listen to the casual reply.
Rocky Mountain high, Colorado.
Rocky Mountain high, Colorado.

Verse 5

Now his life is full of wonder, but his heart still knows some fear
Of a simple thing he cannot comprehend.
Why they try to tear the mountains down to bring in a couple more.
More people, more scars upon the land.

Chorus 3

And the Colorado Rocky Mountain high,
I've seen it rainin' fire in the sky.
I know he'd be a poorer man if he never saw an eagle fly.
Rocky Mountain high, Colorado.
Rocky Mountain high, Colorado.

Outro

Colorado Rocky Mountain high,
I've seen it rainin' fire in the sky.
Friends around the campfire and everybody's high.
‖: Rocky Mountain high, Colorado.   :‖

(Sittin' On) The Dock of the Bay

Words and Music by Steve Cropper
and Otis Redding

Melody:

Sit - tin' in the morn - ing sun, _____

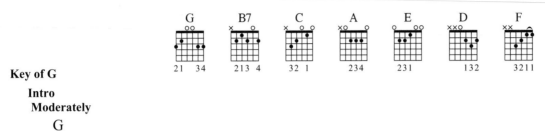

21 34   213 4   32 1   234   231   132   3211

Key of G

Intro
Moderately

G

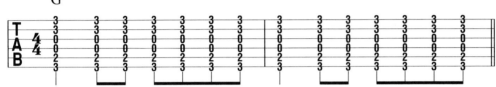

Verse 1

G   B7   C   A
Sittin' in the morning sun, I'll be sittin' when the evening comes.
G   B7   C   A
Watching the ships roll in, then I watch them roll away a-gain.

Chorus

            G   E   G   E
Yeah, I'm sittin' on the dock of the bay, watching the tide roll a-way.
            G   A   G   E
Oo, I'm just sittin' on the dock of the bay, wasting time.

Verse 2

I left my home in Georgia, headed for the 'Frisco Bay.
I have nothing to live for, it looks like nothing's gonna come my way.   ***(Repeat Chorus)***

Bridge

G   D   C   G   D   C
    Looks like nothing's gonna change.   Ev-'rything still remains the same.
G D   C   G   F   D
    I can't do what ten people tell me to do,   so I guess I'll re-main the same, yes.

Verse 3

I'm sittin' here resting my bones, and this loneliness won't leave me alone, yes.
Two thousand miles I roamed just to make this a dock my home.   ***(Repeat Chorus)***

The Sound of Silence

Words and Music by Paul Simon

Melody:

Hel - lo   dark - ness,   my   old   friend,

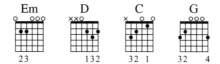

Em   D   C   G

Key of Em

Intro
Moderately

Em

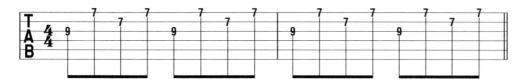

Verse 1

               D   **Em**
Hello darkness, my old friend. I've come to talk with you a-gain.
         C   **G**   **C**   **G**
Because a vision soft-ly creep-ing, left its seeds while I was sleep-ing.
         C   **G**   **Em G**   **D**   **Em**
And the vision that was planted in my brain still re-mains   within the sound of silence.

Verse 2

In restless dreams I walked alone narrow streets of cobblestone.
'Neath the halo of a streetlamp, I turned my collar to the cold and damp.
When my eyes were stabbed by the flash of a neon light that split the night and touched the sound of silence.

Verse 3

And in the naked light I saw ten thousand people, maybe more.
People talking without speaking, people hearing without list'ning.
People writing songs that voices never share. And no one dare disturb the sound of silence.

Verse 4

"Fools!" said I, "You do not know silence like a cancer grows.
Hear my words that I might teach you. Take my arms that I might reach you."
But my words like silent raindrops fell, and echoed in the wells of silence.

Verse 5

And the people bowed and prayed to the neon god they made.
And the sign flashed out its warning. In the words that it was forming.
And the signs said, "The words of the prophets are written on the subway walls and tenement halls."
Whisper the sounds of silence.

Stand by Me

Words and Music by Jerry Leiber,
Mike Stoller and Ben E. King

Melody:

When the   night ____   has come

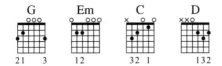

G   Em   C   D

Key of G

Intro
Moderately

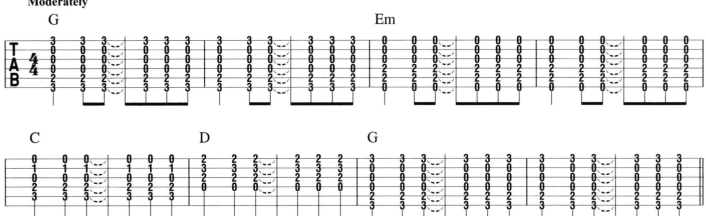

Verse 1

            G   **Em**
When the night has come   and the land is dark
            C   **D**   **G**
And the moon is the only light we'll see.
                       Em
No, I won't be afraid. Oh, I won't be afraid.
            C   **D**   **G**
Just as long as you stand, stand by me.

Chorus

                  G
So darling, darling, stand by me.
  Em
Oh, stand by me.
     C   **D**
Oh, stand,   stand by me.
G
   Stand by me.

Verse 2

If the sky that we look upon should tumble and fall,
Or the mountain should crumble to the sea,
I won't cry, I won't cry. No, I won't shed a tear.
Just as long as you stand, stand by me.   ***(Repeat Chorus)***

Summer Breeze

Words and Music by James Seals
and Dash Crofts

Melody:

See the cur - tains hang - in' in the win - dow

Em   C   E   G   D   A   Am7   Bm7   C/D   D/E   A/B

Key of Em

Intro
Moderately slow

Em   C   Em   C   Em   C   Em   C

Verse 1

E   G   D   A   E   Am7
See the curtains hangin' in the window   in the evening on a Friday night.
E   G   D   A   E
A little light was shinin' through the window.   Lets me know ev'ry-thing's alright.

Chorus

Am7   Bm7   Am7   G
‖: Summer breeze makes me feel fine, blowin' through the jasmine in my mind.   :‖

Interlude

‖: Em   Am7 | Em   Am7 :‖

Verse 2

See the paper layin' on the sidewalk, a little music from the house next door.
So I walked on up to the doorstep, through the screen and across the floor.   *(Repeat Chorus)*

Bridge

Em   Am7   Em   Am7 Em Am7   Em   Am7
Sweet days of summer, the jasmine's in bloom. July is dressed up and playing her tune.
          C/D   D/E   C/D   D/E   A/B
And I come home from a hard day's work and you're waitin' there; not a care in the world.

Verse 3

See the smile a waitin' in the kitchen; food cookin' and the plates for two.
Feel the arms that reach out to hold me in the evening when the day is through.   *(Repeat Chorus)*

Sundown

Words and Music by Gordon Lightfoot

I can see her ly - in' back in her

Key of G

Intro
Moderately slow

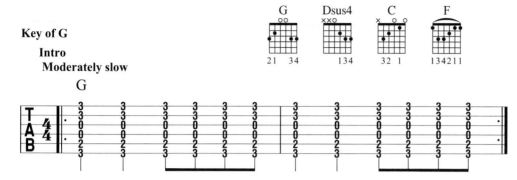

Verse 1

G5
I can see her lyin' back in her satin dress
Dsus4   **G5**
In a room where you do what you don't confess.

Chorus 1

G5   **C**
‖: Sundown, you better take care
    F   **G5**
If I find you been creepin' 'round my back stairs.   :‖

Verse 3

She's been lookin' like a queen in a sailor's dream,
And she don't always say what she really means.

Chorus 2

‖: Sometimes, I think it's a shame
When I get feelin' better when I'm feelin' no pain.   :‖

Verse 3

I can picture ev'ry move that a man could make.
Getting lost in her lovin' is your first mistake.

Chorus 3

Sundown, you better take care
If I find you been creepin' 'round my back stairs.
Sometimes, I think it's a sin
When I feel like I'm winnin' when I'm losin' again.

Verse 4

I can see her lookin' fast in her faded jeans.
She's a hard lovin' woman, got me feelin' mean.

Chorus 4

Sometimes, I think it's a shame
When I get feelin' better when I'm feelin' no pain.
‖: Sundown, you better take care
If I find you been creepin' 'round my back stairs.   :‖
Sometimes I think it's a sin
When I feel like I'm winnin' when I'm losin' again.

Sunshine on My Shoulders

Words by John Denver
Music by John Denver, Mike Taylor and Dick Kniss

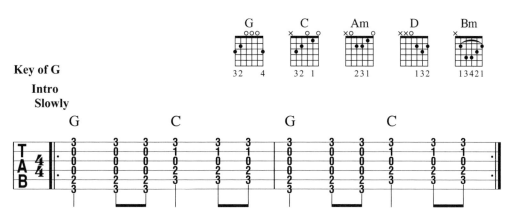

Key of G

Intro
Slowly

| G | C | G | C |

Chorus 1

| G | C | G | C | | G | C | G | C |
Sunshine on my shoulders makes me happy.
| G | C | G | C | | Am | D |
Sunshine in my eyes can make me cry.
| G | C | G | C | | G | C | G | C |
Sunshine on the water looks so lovely.
| G | C | G | C | | G | C | G | C |
Sunshine almost always makes me high.

Verse 1

| G | Am | Bm | C | | G | Am | Bm | C |
If I had a day that I could give you,
| G | Am | Bm | C | | Am | D |
I'd give to you a day just like to-day.
| G | Am | Bm | C | | G | Am | Bm | C |
If I had a song that I could sing for you,
| G | Am | Bm | C | G | Am | Bm | C |
I'd sing a song to make you feel this way. *(Repeat Chorus)*

Verse 2

If I had a tale that I could tell you,
I'd tell a tale sure to make you smile.
If I had a wish that I could wish for you,
I'd make a wish for sunshine all the while.

Chorus 3

Sunshine on my shoulders makes me happy.
Sunshine in my eyes can make me cry.
Sunshine on the water looks so lovely.
Sunshine almost always makes me high.
Sunshine almost all the time makes me high.
Sunshine almost always...

Sweet Caroline

Words and Music by Neil Diamond

Melody:

Where it be - gan, _____

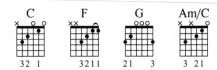

Key of C

Moderately

Verse 1

```
C                      F
   Where it began,      I can't begin to knowin',
C                               G
   But then I know it's growin' strong.
C                      F
   Was in the spring,     and spring became the summer.
C                               G
   Who'd have believed you'd come a-long?
C        Am/C
Hands,      touchin' hands.
G                F                        G
   Reachin' out,     touchin' me, touchin' you.
```

Chorus

```
C          F
Sweet Caro-line,
                         G
Good times never seemed so good.
C          F                        G
I've been in-clined to believe they never would. But now I...
```

Verse 2

```
Look at the night and it don't seem so lonely;
We fill it up with only two.
And when I hurt, hurtin' runs off my shoulders.
How can I hurt when holding you?
Warm, touching warm.
Reachin' out, touchin' me, touchin' you.    (Repeat Chorus)
```

Sweet Home Alabama

Words and Music by Ronnie Van Zant,
Ed King and Gary Rossington

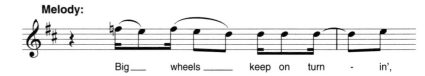

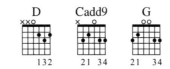

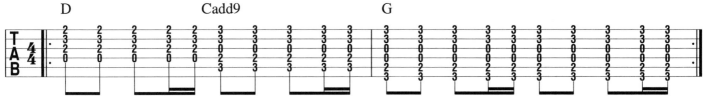

Key of D

Intro
Moderately

Verse 1

D   Cadd9   G
Big wheels keep on turnin',
D   Cadd9   G
Carry me home to see my kin.
D   Cadd9   G
Singin' songs about the southland.
D   Cadd9   G
I miss old 'Bamee once a-gain.   *(Repeat Intro)*

Verse 2

Well, I heard Mister Young sing about her.
Well, I heard old Neil put her down.
Well, I hope Neil Young will remember,
A southern man don't need him around anyhow.

Chorus

D   Cadd9   G
Sweet home Ala-bama,
D   Cadd9   G
Where the skies are so blue.
D   Cadd9   G
Sweet home Ala-bama,
D   Cadd9   G
Lord, I'm comin' home to you.   *(Repeat Intro)*

Verse 3

In Birmingham they love the gov'nor, boo boo, hoo.
Now we all did what we could do.
Now Watergate does not bother me,
Does your conscience bother you? Tell the truth.   *(Repeat Intro)*

Verse 4

Now, Muscle Shoals has got the Swampers
An' they been known to pick a song or two. (Yes, they do!)
Lord, they get me off so much,
They pick me up when I'm feelin' blue 'n' how 'bout you?   *(Repeat Chorus)*

Take Me Home, Country Roads

Words and Music by John Denver,
Bill Danoff and Taffy Nivert

Melody:

Al - most   heav - en,___

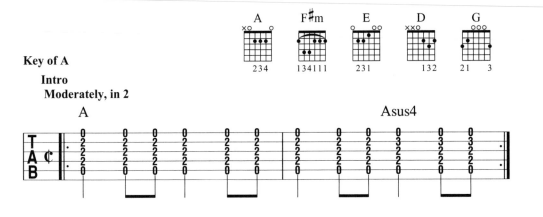

Key of A

Intro
Moderately, in 2

Verse 1

  A   **F♯m**
    Almost heaven,   West Virginia,
E   **D**   **A**
    Blue Ridge Mountains, Shenandoah River.
            F♯m
    Life is old there, older than the trees,
E   **D**   **A**
    Younger than the mountains, growin' like a breeze.

Chorus

       A   **E**
    Country roads, take me home
   F♯m   **D**
    To the place I be-long.
       A   **E**
    West Vir-ginia, mountain momma.
    D   **A**
    Take me home, country roads.

Verse 2

    All my mem'ries gather 'round her,
    Miner's lady, stranger to blue water.
    Dark and dusty, painted on the sky,
    Misty taste of moonshine, teardrop in my eye.   *(Repeat Chorus)*

Bridge

F♯m   **E**   **A**
    I hear her voice, in the mornin' hour she calls me.
    D   **A**   **E**
    The radio re-minds me of my home far away.
    F♯m   **G**   **D**
    And drivin' down the road I get a feeling
    A   **E**
    That I should have been home yesterday. Yesterday. *(Repeat Chorus)*

Teach Your Children

Words and Music by Graham Nash

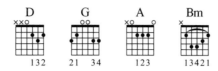

Key of D

Intro
Moderately fast, in 2

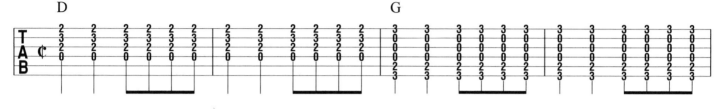

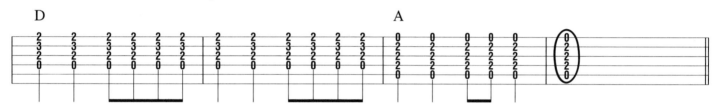

Verse 1

```
 D              G              D          A
You, who are on the road, must have a code that you can live by.
 D              G              D          A
And so become your-self, because the past is just a goodbye.
```

Chorus 1

```
 D              G              D          A
Teach your children well. Their father's hell did slowly go by.
    D           G              D              A
And feed them on your dreams; the one they picks, the one you'll know by.
 D                    G                      D
   Don't you ever ask them why. If they told you, you would cry.
                    Bm    G    A          D
So just look at them and sigh       and know they love you.
```

Verse 2

```
And you, of tender years, can't know the fears that your elders grew by.
And so, please help them with your youth. They seek the truth before they can die.
```

Chorus 2

```
Teach your parents well. Their children's hell will slowly go by.
And feed them on your dreams; the one they pick, the one you'll go by.
Don't you ever ask them why. If they told you, you would cry.
So just look at them and sigh and know they love you.
```

49

This Land Is Your Land

Words and Music by Woody Guthrie

Melody:

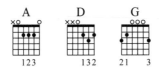

This land is your land...

A   D   G

123 132 21 3

Key of D

Intro
Moderately fast, in 2

A   D

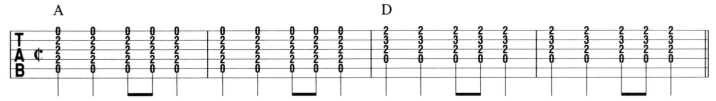

Chorus

                 G   **D**   **A**   **D**

This land is your land and this land is my land from Cali-fornia to the New York island.

                 G   **D**   **A**   **D**

From the redwood forest to the Gulf Stream waters, this land was made for you and me.

Verse 1

                 G   **D**   **A**   **D**

As I was walking that ribbon of highway, I saw a-bove me that endless skyway,

                 G   **D**   **A**   **D**

I saw be-low me that golden valley. This land was made for you and me.

Verse 2

I've roamed and rambled and I followed my footsteps to the sparkling sands of her diamond deserts.
All around me, a voice was sounding: this land was made for you and me.

Verse 3

When the sun came shining, and I was strolling, and the wheat fields waving, and the dust clouds rolling,
As the fog was lifting a voice was chanting: "This land was made for you and me."   *(Repeat Chorus)*

Verse 4

As I went walking, I saw a sign there, and on the sign it said, "No Trespassing."
But on the other side it didn't say nothing. This side was made for you and me.

Verse 5

In the shadow of the steeple I saw my people, by the relief office I seen my people;
As they stood there hungry, I stood there asking: Is this land made for you and me?

Verse 6

Nobody living can ever stop me, as I go walking that freedom highway;
Nobody living can ever make me turn back. This land was made for you and me.   *(Repeat Chorus)*

Wagon Wheel

Words and Music by Bob Dylan
and Ketch Secor

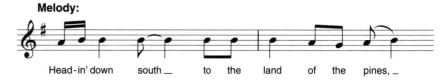

Melody:

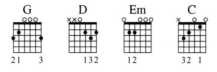

Head-in' down south to the land of the pines,

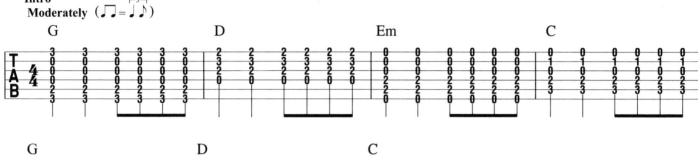

G   D   Em   C

Key of G

Intro
Moderately

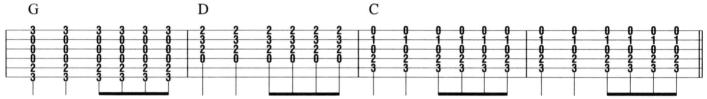

Verse 1

G	D	Em	C

Headin' down south to the land of the pines, I'm thumbin' my way out of North Caroline.

G	D	C	G	D

Starin' up the road and pray to God I see headlights. I made it down the coast in seventeen hours.

Em	C	G	D	C

Pickin' me a bouquet of dogwood flowers. And I'm hopin' for Raleigh; I can see my baby to-night.

Chorus

G	D	Em	C

So rock me, mama, like a wagon wheel. Rock me, mama, any way you feel.

G D   **C**   **G**   **D**

Hey,   mama, rock me. Rock me, mama, like the wind and the rain.

Em   **C**   **G D**   **C**

Rock me, mama, like a southbound train. Hey,   mama, rock me.

Verse 2

Runnin' from the cold up in New England, I was born to be a fiddler in an old time string band.
My baby plays the guitar, I pick a banjo now. Oh, north country winters keep a gettin' me down.
Lost my money playin' poker, so I had to leave town.
But I ain't turnin' back to livin' that old life no more.   ***(Repeat Chorus)***

Verse 3

Walkin' through the South out of Roanoke, I caught a trucker out of Philly, had a nice long toke.
But he's a-headin' west from the Cumberland Gap to Johnson City, Tennessee.
I got, I gotta move on before the sun. I hear my baby callin' my name and I know that she's the only one.
And if I die in Raleigh, at least I will die free.   ***(Repeat Chorus)***

Wanted Dead or Alive

Words and Music by Jon Bon Jovi and Richie Sambora

Melody:

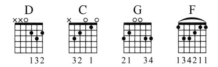

It's all the same, _

D
xx0
132

C
x o o
32 1

G
oo
21 34

F
134211

Key of D

Moderately

Verse 1

   D   C   G
It's all the same; only the names will change.
C   G   F D
Ev'ryday   it seems we're wast-ing a-way.
   D   C   G
A-nother place where the faces are so cold.
   C   G   F D
I'd drive all night just to get back home.

Chorus

     C   G
I'm a cowboy,
       F   D
On a steel horse I ride.
    C   G F   D
I'm wanted   dead or a-live.
C   G F   D
Wanted,   dead or a-live.

Verse 2

Sometimes I sleep, sometimes it's not for days.
The people I meet always go their sep'rate ways.
Sometimes you tell the day by the bottle that you drink.
And times when you're alone, all you do is think.   ***(Repeat Chorus)***

Verse 3

And I walk these streets, a loaded six string on my back.
I play for keeps, 'cause I might not make it back.
I've been ev'rywhere, still I'm standing tall,
I've seen a million faces, and I've rocked them all.   ***(Repeat Chorus)***

Wellerman

New Zealand Folksong

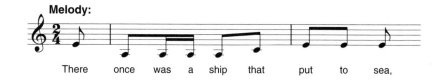

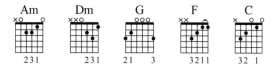

Key of Am

Moderately

Verse 1

     Am   **Dm**   **Am**

There once was a ship that put to sea, and the name of the ship was the Billy of Tea.

                             G   **Am**

The winds blew hard, her bow tipped down. Blow, my bully boys, blow.

Chorus

  F   **C**   **G**   **Am**

Soon may the Wellerman come to bring us sugar and tea and rum.

  F   **C**   **G**   **Am**

One day when the tonguin' is done, we'll take our leave and go.

Verse 2

She had not been two weeks from the shore when down on her a right whale bore.
The captain called all hands and swore he'd take that whale in tow. *(Repeat Chorus)*

Verse 3

Before the boat had hit the water, the whale's tail came up and caught her.
All hands to the side, harpooned and fought her when she dived down below. *(Repeat Chorus)*

Verse 4

No line was cut, no whale was freed. The Captain's mind was not of greed,
But he belonged to the whaleman's creed. She took the ship in tow. *(Repeat Chorus)*

Verse 5

For forty days or even more, the line went slack, then tight once more.
All boats were lost (there were only four), but still the whale did go. *(Repeat Chorus)*

Verse 6

As far as I've heard, the fight's still on. The line's not cut and the whale's not gone.
The Wellerman makes his regular call to encourage the Captain, crew and all. *(Repeat Chorus)*

You Are My Sunshine

Words and Music by Jimmie Davis

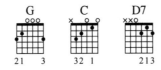

G   C   D7

Key of G

Moderately, in 2

Verse 1

         G
The other night, dear, as I lay sleeping,
        C   **G**
I dreamed I held you in my arms.
        C   **G**
When I a-woke, dear, I was mis-taken,
       D7   **G**
And I hung my head and cried:

Chorus

         G
You are my sunshine, my only sunshine,
        C   **G**
You make me happy when skies are gray.
        C   **G**
You'll never know, dear, how much I love you.
       D7   **G**
Please don't take my sunshine a-way.

Verse 2

I'll always love you and make you happy,
If you will only say the same.
But if you leave me to love another,
You'll regret it all some day.   *(Repeat Chorus)*

Verse 3

You told me once, dear, you really loved me,
And no one else could come between.
But now you've left me and love another;
You have shattered all my dreams.   *(Repeat Chorus)*

RHYTHM TAB LEGEND

Rhythm Tab is a form of notation that adds rhythmic values to the traditional tab staff.

TABLATURE graphically represents the guitar fingerboard. Each horizontal line represents a string, and each number represents a fret. Rhythmic values are shown using ovals, stems, and dots.

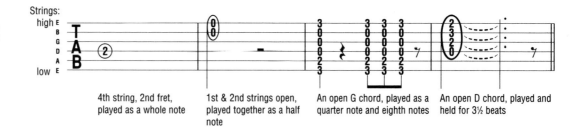

4th string, 2nd fret, played as a whole note

1st & 2nd strings open, played together as a half note

An open G chord, played as a quarter note and eighth notes

An open D chord, played and held for 3½ beats

Definitions for Special Guitar Notation

HALF-STEP BEND: Strike the note and bend up 1/2 step.

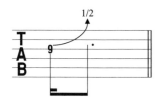

WHOLE-STEP BEND: Strike the note and bend up one step.

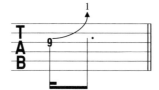

SLIGHT (MICROTONE) BEND: Strike the note and bend up 1/4 step.

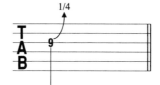

BEND AND RELEASE: Strike the note and bend up as indicated, then release back to the original note. Only the first note is struck.

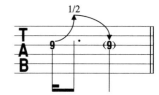

PRE-BEND: Bend the note as indicated, then strike it.

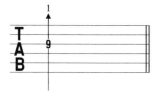

GRACE NOTE PRE-BEND AND RELEASE: Bend the note as indicated. Strike it and release the bend back to the original note.

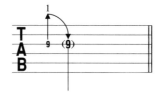

UNISON BEND: Strike the two notes simultaneously and bend the lower note up to the pitch of the higher.

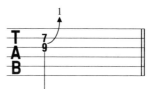

HOLD BEND: While sustaining bent note, strike note on different string.

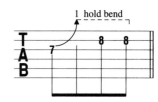

VIBRATO: The string is vibrated by rapidly bending and releasing the note with the fretting hand.

WIDE VIBRATO: The pitch is varied to a greater degree by vibrating with the fretting hand.

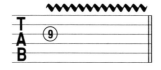

HAMMER-ON: Strike the first (lower) note with one finger, then sound the higher note (on the same string) with another finger by fretting it without picking.

PULL-OFF: Place both fingers on the notes to be sounded. Strike the first note and without picking, pull the finger off to sound the second (lower) note.

HAMMER FROM NOWHERE: Sound note(s) by hammering with fret hand finger only.

GRACE NOTE SLUR: Strike the note and immediately hammer-on (or pull-off) as indicated.

GRACE NOTE SLUR (CLUSTER): Strike the notes and immediately hammer-on (or pull-off) as indicated.

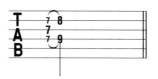

LEGATO SLIDE: Strike the first note and then slide the same fret-hand finger up or down to the second note. The second note is not struck.

SHIFT SLIDE: Same as legato slide, except the second note is struck.

GRACE NOTE SLIDE: Quickly slide into the note from below or above.

TRILL: Very rapidly alternate between the notes indicated by continuously hammering on and pulling off.

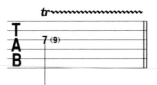

TAPPING: Hammer ("tap") the fret indicated with the pick-hand index or middle finger and pull off to the note fretted by the fret hand.

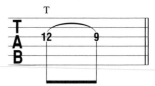

NATURAL HARMONIC: Strike the note while the fret-hand lightly touches the string directly over the fret indicated.

Harm.

PINCH HARMONIC: The note is fretted normally and a harmonic is produced by adding the edge of the thumb or the tip of the index finger of the pick hand to the normal pick attack.

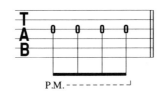

P.H.

HARP HARMONIC: The note is fretted normally and a harmonic is produced by gently resting the pick hand's index finger directly above the indicated fret (in parentheses) while the pick hand's thumb or pick assists by plucking the appropriate string.

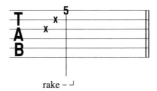

H.H.

PICK SCRAPE: The edge of the pick is rubbed down (or up) the string, producing a scratchy sound.

P.S.

MUFFLED STRINGS: A percussive sound is produced by laying the fret hand across the string(s) without depressing, and striking them with the pick hand.

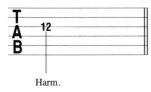

PALM MUTING: The note is partially muted by the pick hand lightly touching the string(s) just before the bridge.

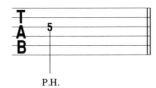

P.M. - - - - - - - - -

RAKE: Drag the pick across the strings indicated with a single motion.

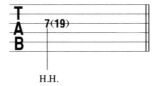

rake - ⌐

TREMOLO PICKING: The note is picked as rapidly and continuously as possible.

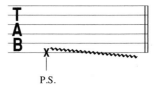

ARPEGGIATE: Play the notes of the chord indicated by quickly rolling them from bottom to top.

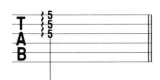

VIBRATO BAR DIVE AND RETURN: The pitch of the note or chord is dropped a specified number of steps (in rhythm), then returned to the original pitch.

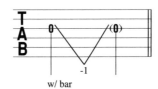

w/ bar

VIBRATO BAR SCOOP: Depress the bar just before striking the note, then quickly release the bar.

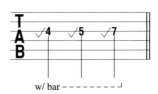

w/ bar - - - - - - - ⌐

VIBRATO BAR DIP: Strike the note and then immediately drop a specified number of steps, then release back to the original pitch.

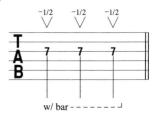

w/ bar - - - - - - - ⌐

Additional Musical Definitions

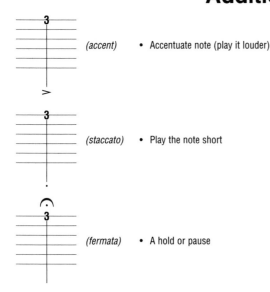

(accent) • Accentuate note (play it louder)

(staccato) • Play the note short

(fermata) • A hold or pause

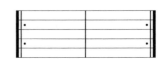

┌┐ • Downstroke

V • Upstroke

• Repeat measures between signs

NOTE: Tablature numbers in parentheses are used when:
  • The note is sustained, but a new articulation begins (such as a hammer-on, pull-off, slide, or bend), or
  • A bend is released.
  • A note sustains while crossing from one staff to another.